MAY DAY IN NOTTINGHAMSHIRE

by

FRANK EARP

Heart of Albion Press

© Text and illustrations copyright Frank E. Earp 1991
All rights reserved

This publication may not be reproduced in whole or in part in any manner whatsoever without written permission except in the case of brief quotations embodied in critical articles or reviews.

Printed in England by
Newark Chamber of Commerce
Printing and Graphic Design Department

ISBN 1 872883 13 3

Heart of Albion Press
2, Cross Hill Close, Wymeswold,
Loughborough, LE12 6UJ
Telephone (0509) 880725

Introduction

> *And when the merrie merrie May is done,*
> *When on Bel Hill the fires are seen to glow,*
> *Maypole is up, and Marris is begun,*
> *Beware, O foolish people, what ye do!*
> *Forget not blessed Aidan's name*
> *To Holy Church be true.*

The above lines are the second verse of a poem by Agnes M. Alford, entitled 'A Medieval May Day, (The Vicar's Admonation)'. I do not know when or where it was first published, I found it on the frontispiece of a book on *English Folk Dance* by Violet Alford, published in 1923. I have chosen it to open my own booklet because I feel it encapsulates the whole history and tradition of May Day. From the bright Beltane fires burning throughout the night on May Eve, to the tall Maypole on the village green with its attendant Morris Men and even the condemnation of the Church authorities, are all to be found within these pages relating to May Day in Nottinghamshire.

May Day was once one of the most important days in the calendar year. Little is now left of its former glory, here and there we find far-flung remnants, isolated customs and traditions. Because of its standing in former times enough written material survives for us to build up a complete picture of May Day as it once was. Records and historical documents tell us that Nottinghamshire once had ten permanent Maypoles including Wellow, many of them surviving in situ until the end of the last century. However, May Day was not just about Maypoles and Maypole-dancing. To understand the events that took place annually on 1st May we must first learn something of the history of May Day.

A brief history of May Day Nottinghamshire and elsewhere

Whatever May Day has now become, one thing is certain, it was once an important pre-christian religious festival. Much of what we now regard as 'charming folk customs' had their origins in such ancient festivals. We cannot be certain when May Day took on religious significance, but there is considerable evidence to show that neolithic and bronze age man marked the rising of the sun on 1st May with alignments of monoliths and earth mounds. This need to mark the sunrise on a precise day may only have been a device for setting a calendar, but it is more likely to have contained deep religious significance. The Romans called the fifth month of the year 'Maia' in honour of the goddess of growth and increase (from which is derived our modern May). It is to the Romans that some scholars attribute many of our present May Day customs. The Saxons called the month Thrimilci, quite simply, the month in which cows can be milked three times a day. It is from the Saxon association of May with milk, that the 'Milk Maids Dance' may have had its origin.

1:   Milkmaid's dance (from Chamber's Book of Days, 1869)

In many parts of the country, including Nottinghamshire, 'milk maids' would arise early in the morning on 1st May and after performing certain ritual ablutions,

A fair maid who, the first of May
Goes to the fields at break of day
And washes in dew from the hawthorn tree
Will ever after handsome be.
(Folk Rhyme, Anon.)

they then would, proceed to dance in the streets of their town or village, balancing on their heads as many containers of milk as they could manage. There are also a number of May carols and folk songs containing references to milk and cream and dairy maids.

It is to the pre-christian Celts that we must turn to understand the full significance of May Day. To the Celts, May Day, or more precisely, 1st May, was Beltane, the middle of their calendar year. Beltane was one of the quarter days each of which was celebrated by the lighting of great bonfires on prominent hills. Such was the importance of these fires that the name 'beltane' translates as

'Bel' - bright or goodly, and 'tan' - fire; Violet Alford mentions the Bel Hill in her verse and Nottinghamshire as a city had its own Bel Hill. It was to St Anne's and St Anne's Well that the people of Nottingham led by their mayor and council would process to celebrate May Day. This prominent hill rising above the city would have been an ideal Bel Hill. The well at St Anne's is generally regarded as being a pre-christian Holy Well. Where pre-christian holy sites are rededicated to St Anne, Whitlock and other folklorists tell us that St Anne is likely to be a corruption of 'San' - holy and 'Tan' - fire.

There is in the history of Nottinghamshire a direct reference to the lighting of a Bel Fire. Writing at the beginning of the last century, Dr Spencer T. Hall describes just such an event. In an account concerning the Hemlock Stone, a massive sandstone outcrop at Bramcote, he says '... the lighting of a fire upon it annually on Beltane Eve, as old people in my young days could remember and describe...'. As can be seen from this quote, it was traditional to begin celebrations on the eve of May Day. This custom has also been passed to us via the Celts. It is, however, something that they themselves inherited from earlier times, a practice that meant that the celebrants were able to witness the rising of the sun on the holy day. Hall's account also strengthens the connection between ancient stones and May Day. Although Nottinghamshire has no stones officially classified as monoliths, it does have a number of natural stones such as the Hemlock Stone that have ancient traditions associated with them. Using one such stone, the Cat Stone at Strelley, a few miles north of the Hemlock Stone, the author has discovered a Beltane Sunrise alignment terminating on a Bel Hill - Sunrise Hill, Bestwood. This line has been dated between 1800 and 1700 BC. A second Beltane Sunrise line (also discovered by the author) exists at Blidworth. In a field not far from the church is a massive conglomerate outcrop known as the 'Druid Stone'. The stone has an artificial cave cut into its south - western side, with an aperture opening out of the far wall. The ground on the north-eastern side of the stone rises to a flat ridge and when viewed through the aperture in the stone presents an almost horizontal horizon sky line. The aperture is so designed as to force a view in a set direction to the summit of the ridge and an isolated boulder. This line of site has been speculated upon by early antiquarians (Deering for one) as being a mid-summer sunrise line. It is in fact a May Day sunrise once again dated at between 1800 and 1700 BC.

Another ancient custom associated with May Day mentioned in the county records and elsewhere is the 'bringing in' or 'bringing home of the May'. It was once a widespread custom for couples to go off together into the woods on May Eve, 'there to make merrie sport'. On their return at dawn on May Day they would carry bunches of greenery and whitethorn blossom, known as 'May Blossom'. Those young men who had not paired off in the night would go around the village or town leaving sprays of such greenery at the doors of various houses for the attention of the female occupants. each kind of tree or shrub had a meaning, as the old rhyme says;

'Nut for a slut; plum for the glum
Bramble if she ramble; Gorse for the whores.'

It would seem that the expression "say it with flowers" is not a new one. These 'May Bushes' as they were known, have been attributed to the Romans who gathered greenery on 1st May in honour of the goddess Flora. However, where thorn blossom is concerned, the origin may well lie in Celtic 'Cult of the Thorn'. It was traditional to place a spray of such blossoms above the outside door of a house or cow shed to guard against evil and bring good luck. This spray remained over the door until the following May Day, when it would be replaced. It was however, bad luck to take thorn blossoms, particularly black thorn, into the house, a superstition and belief still to be found in many parts of the county

A common part of the May Day celebrations in many parts of the country was the 'Robin Hood Games'. It is not surprising that in a county that claims Robin as its own, these games were very popular. Such games naturally enough contained displays of archery but, more importantly, Robin Hood became the focal point for the May Day celebrations as a whole. He was seen as the consort and protector of the May Queen, although later to be replaced by the May King. In May Games Robin Hood, the Outlaw, appears to have taken on the personification of the spirit of the forest. He was 'Jack-in-the-Green', the Green Man, the spirit of vegetation that is awakened each year in spring. So complete did this identity change become, any historical personage is lost in a morass of mythology. Whatever the true identity of Robin Hood, so powerful was his association with May Day that in 1549, Bishop Latimar felt compelled to preach a sermon on the subject before none other than the King himself, Edward VI. Robin's popularity at May Day celebrations prompted the custom of hanging portraits of the hero and his merry men in the streets and more importantly, from the Maypole (see Gotham, in the Maypole gazetteer).

Finally, we come to the Maypole, that most famous of all symbols of May Day. The Maypole has a long and noble history that takes it back at least as far as the ancient sunrise lines discussed earlier. In general, the Maypole has survived in this country in two distinct forms. By far the most widespread is the short, continental-style pole around which we see children dancing and plaiting coloured ribbons. This form of pole and dancing is said to have been introduced into this country in 1888, by John Ruskin. The English Maypoles, now a rarity are usually permanent features of the landscape and are extremely tall. More will be said about the Maypole generally at the beginning of the Maypole gazetteer section, which contain entries for Nottinghamshire's permanent English Maypoles.

The Celebrations

As we have already noted the May Day celebrations did not just revolve around the Maypole and Maypole dancing. From council records and other historical documents, we find that Nottinghamshire once enjoyed an active and eventful May Day. Such activities recorded for Nottinghamshire are typical of celebrations taking place throughout the country and reflect the attitudes and tastes of their time. Again, as we have seen, many of the customs and traditions were very ancient and served a social and religious function. Although their original meaning has all but been forgotten and in spite of suppression by religious zealots, these customs continued to enjoy popular approval and many have survived into our own time.

Maypoles were often erected on traditional sites and likewise we find that other May Day celebrations had ancient, traditional sites as focal points for the activity. Once again we find Nottingham as a city was no exception to this. As we have seen, it was to St Anne's Well that the people of Nottingham, would parade in order to celebrate May Day. St Anne's Well was also the site of other celebration such as Easter Monday, etc. As the eighteenth century historian Deering puts it, the parade to this venue was 'By a custom time beyond memory'.

2:   *Elizabethan Maypole (from Chamber's Book of Days, 1869)*

THE CELEBRATIONS

From the surviving records, these celebrations must have been noisy and spectacular events. As well as the obligatory Morris dancers, the' town waits' (band) led the assembled company to the well. Again, from the records we find that great quantities of gunpowder were used, doubtless to the same effect as our modern fireworks. Although there is no mention of such, we may imagine a large bonfire to have been set up and, perhaps even more likely, a Maypole. We also find reference to the 'Robin Hood Games' in early manuscripts and in the works of later historians like Briscoe. We do not know what sort of celebrations accompanied the lighting of the Beltane fire on top of the Hemlock Stone, we may guess that they would be similar to those at St Anne's but on a smaller scale.

Let us look then at some of the written evidence in the form of extracts from the county records and try to get a flavour of May Day festivities in bygone Nottinghamshire.

Our earliest reference comes from the reign of Henry VIII, a king who himself enjoyed greatly the May Day celebrations:

1541:- The town funds were charged with 16d paid for wine on May Day when we rode May and also given to Master Stapleton and in other ways.
Also with 8d given to Master Thomas Skevynton when he and other young men brought in May of May Day with Master Mayor.

1569:- Nottingham chamberlains paid 4s to the waits for playing to St Anne's Well the Monday in Easter week before the mayor and for May Day. And 6s 8d 'reward gevyn unto the Daunsers that bought in May. With 10s, at the same time to gunners and for powder'.

1572:- The town paid 24s to gunners, dancers and others that took pains and for gunpowder on the Sunday after May Day. In the same year 1s 4d was paid for gunpowder and match and 2s for setting the Watch and 18d for two men going with their drums.

1573:- 21s given in reward on May Day to gunners, dancers and others and for 5lbs of gunpowder.

1575:- £3 2s 6d was spent on bringing in the May Day at Nottingham.

1576:- 10s was paid 'unto serteyne daunsers and others that dyd bringe in Maye before Maister on Sunday after May Day'.

1579:- 9s 4d paid for 8lbs of gunpowder and 8s was also 'gevyn to daunsers' at the 'brygeng in of May'.

1588:- 6d paid to the Stapleford who came with a May Game (Robin Hood Game).

By this last date the May Day celebrants were beginning to fall foul of the growing puritanical laws which almost eradicated all such festivities in the time of the Commonwealth (see also Broughton Maypole). Laws were now being passed that made attendance at church services on a Sunday obligatory. The liberal view which tolerated the celebration of a pagan festival like May Day on a Sunday were also being challenged, as we can see from the final two extracts;

1605:- Peter Roos of Laxton admitted that he was participating in 'the maye game' during service time on the Sabbath day.

1608:- May Day fell on a Sunday and despite the law as to the attendance at church, there was a football match on the Meadows (an area of Nottingham) during service time. The players appear to have escaped, but eleven men who where caught returning from watching the game were prosecuted.

We do not know what happened to Peter Roos or to the eleven football fans, but from other records of the time we find that a number of Morris Men who were caught dancing on a Sunday were given heavy fines.

J. Potter Briscoe in *Nottingham Fact and Fiction*, 1876, tells us of May Day activities in other parts of the county: 'It was usual at Edwinstowe, and no doubt at many other villages in this county, on May mornings, for youth of both sexes to hie themselves to the forest and gather token flowers and branches before day, and return with them, with accompaniments of music and all signs of merriment, to decorate the doors and windows of their lovers and neighbours before they were up in the morning'. Briscoe goes on to say that this custom had long since died out, and, 'Not content with this, these merry people had in every town and village a fixed pole, to which, on Mayday the suspended wreaths of flowers'. To what extent Briscoe was referring to specific Maypoles when he made this statement, we can only guess. He also informs us that Nottinghamshire had its own 'Milk Maids Dance' on May Day.

May Day celebrations continued to be enjoyed by Nottinghamshire folk well into our own times, but these were mainly centred on the number of permanent Maypoles scatted throughout the county. As we will see, these poles slowly disappeared and with them the remaining celebrations. Nottinghamshire now has only one remaining permanent Maypole at Wellow and celebrations still take place around it every year on the May Bank Holiday.

For the last five years the Foresters Morris Men from Nottingham have revived an ancient May Day custom by dancing at dawn on 1st May. This takes place around 5.15 a.m. on the eminence above the city up on which stands Nottingham Castle, popularly called 'Castle Rock'. This modern revival shows that there is still an interest in traditional folk customs and a number of such events such as May Fairs take place throughout the county but, often as not, these events now take place after 1st May and many may no longer be classified as true May Day celebrations.

The Maypole

> *But the chiefest jewel they bring from thence is their May-pole, which they bring home with great veneration, as thus. They have twentie or fortie yoke of oxen, every oxe having a sweet nose-gay of flouers placed on the tip of his hornes, and these oxen drawe home this May-pole (this stynkyng ydol, rather), which is covered all over with flouers and hearbs, bound round about with strings, from top to the bottome, and sometimes painted with variable colours.*
> Phillip Stubbes, The anatomie of Abuses, 1583.

It is a surprising fact that often the most virulent opponent of an event offers us the best description. Such is the case with the Maypole. By the end of the sixteenth century May Day celebration and in particular, the nocturnal visits to the woods and the Maypole itself, were coming under increasing attack from the growing force of religious zealots and puritans like Stubbes. This tide of religious fervour was eventually to lead to the bloodshed of the Civil War. In the case of one Nottinghamshire pole (Gedling), it was to lead to the longest and perhaps the strangest case in British legal history. What was it about May Day that provoked such outrage and indignation in Stubbes and his fellows? For over a thousand years, paganism and christianity had existed side by side, in a sort of symbiotic relationship. Now, with the new order, all things 'papish and pagan' were considered intolerable. The Maypole, standing in its prominent position on the village green, often within sight of the church and sometimes even in the church yard, was an obvious target. It represented the very height of paganism and idolatry. As Briscoe says, perhaps with some slight exaggeration, '..every town and village had such a pole'. In 1644 an order was given by Parliament for all Maypoles to be taken down. With the exception of a few rural villages, this order was carried out and many Maypoles that had stood for generations were to vanish forever.

3: Clifton Maypole (undated, c.1905-10) with the head joiner and gardeners from Clifton Hall responsible for its erection (courtesy Nottinghamshire County Libraries).

What is a Maypole, what does it symbolise? This is a complicated issue which cannot be explored in any detail here. The Maypole is one of those objects that can be all things to all men. To say that it is merely a phallic symbol is to demean its long history. Tall, slender, upright poles either singular or arranged in a pattern have been venerated as religious objects in this country for thousands of years. Such poles have been shown to pre-date the megaliths mentioned earlier. It is extremely likely that these prehistoric poles were the ancestors of today's Maypole. There is evidence to show that an element of tree worship is involved with both the ancestral poles and the Maypole, but then again to say that this is the entire answer would be wrong. It is clear that, as with monoliths and later crosses, the site upon which the Maypole was erected was most important. In the case of two Nottinghamshire Maypoles, Linby and Stapleford (and several others throughout the country), they were erected so close to the base of the village cross as to make dancing around them all but impossible. Unlike the Bel Fires, the Maypole occupies a site within a town or village, often close to a site of religious importance, one might say at its very heart. This venerated spot can only be seen as synonymous with the local omphalos. Beltane was not only the middle of the Celtic year, it was considered to be the pivot or turning point of the year about which all revolves. The Maypole can thus be seen as the physical enbodyment of this turning point, the axis mundi, the point around which the whole universe revolves. It is somewhat symbolic that iconographically the axis of the world, the north and south poles, are seen in our minds as poles painted with a red and white spiral, exactly like a Maypole.

Nottinghamshire's Permanent Maypoles

'....the dance beneath the May-pole, where is it?'
William Howitt, 1865.

Nottinghamshire has only one surviving permanent Maypole of any antiquity, (it had a second, modern pole at Woodborough). With this one exception all the other poles listed here have now, sadly, disappeared. Some of the references are very short as the original quotes are almost accidental recordings of such and such a village or town having a pole. The county may indeed have had many more Maypoles that were unfortunate enough to disappear without such a reference recorded for prosperity. There may even be obscure references waiting to be discovered. Writing in a letter to the *Nottingham Guardian*, in 1914, Thomas Ratcliffe of Worksop says that his grandmother had told him many years previously that in her childhood; '....morris dances, mummers and dancing about the maypole were fairly common in all country places'.

Gazetteer

Grid references are from O.S. sheets 129 and 120. Where the exact location of a pole has not been recorded, I have given the grid reference of the parish church or central location.

Bradmore. (Church; Sheet 129 SK 58403115)

Bradmore is a small hamlet, some six miles south of the city of Nottingham. It has a possible tumulus, an ancient chapel and once had a permanent Maypole. George Pryn who went to live in the neighbouring village of Bunny in 1792 writes in his autobiography that he saw; '....the maypole at Broadmore, (Bradmore) and the people dancing round it. It was made so that it could be lowered to the ground to be dressed with flowers, and raised up again'. We do not know how long the Maypole had been standing in Bradmore, or how long after the above date it remained so. One thing is certain however, with such a intricate mechanism, it is extremely likely that the pole had been in use for a number of years. May Day might well have been celebrated in Bradmore two hundred years earlier. In 1618, the church courts cracked down on Morris dancing on Sundays and a number of men were fined for this offence, among them were men from Bradmore.

Boughton (Church; Sheet 120 SK 67856850)

There is no evidence to support the idea that Boughton ever had a permanent Maypole. In fact, there is but a single reference to Boughton ever possessing a Maypole. I have included this reference because it once again, clearly, demonstrates the attitude of the church to the underlying paganism of the Maypole and the common peoples response, in erecting Stubbes's 'stynkyng ydol' on its very doorstep. Church court records show that on 16th October, 1585, Robert Dewych of Boughton was cited in that; 'he did set up a Maypole in ye church yard'. We do not know the outcome of the case, or if the incident occurred in May, why it took six months to bring the action to court. It may have been that a number of people were involved and Dewych was merely a 'scapegoat' or even the ring leader. I would like to believe that he/they were setting up a pole on a traditional site that had been used before, or even replacing a decaying pole, but we will never know. (See also Gedling Maypole).

4:     Clifton Maypole dancing in 1937 (courtesy of Mr K . Cooper).

Clifton (Pole; Sheet 129 SK 54703476)

Clifton is one of the many villages about which it has been said; 'had a Maypole since time immemorial'. This statement was repeated in local papers in May 1937, when we read that; '.... a revival of braiding the village maypole at Clifton has been made'. It may have been the Maypole that attracted the teenagers and young people of the 18th century when it was popular for young people to take the ferry from Nottingham over to Clifton (there was no Clifton bridge then of course) to spend the day in 'merry pastimes' on the village green and walking the length of Clifton Grove. Complaints were made by villagers to local government about the 'noise, nuisance and lateness of those returning home in the evening'. This prompted the familiar cry of 'What is our youth coming to?' However, not all the locals complained and it proved a lucrative trade in teas and other refreshments.

A probable Maypole, tea shops and a pleasant walk along Clifton's wooded 'Grove' were not the only attractions Clifton had to offer. Clifton village green also had a turf cut maze. The only information we have about this maze comes from Thoresby's revised edition of Robert Thoroton's Antiquities of Nottingham' where a (reversed) plan of the maze is included in the material relating to the Shepherd's Race, a turf maze at Sneinton, '.....on the summit of a hill near St.

Anne's Well'. Although the origin of such mazes is somewhat shrouded in mystery, they are believed to be very ancient and, like the Maypole, to have been part of the pre-Christian religion. It is interesting to note that what may have been a Bel Hill at Sneinton was crowned with a maze, while the Maypole site at Clifton also had a maze close by. The Grove mentioned earlier, although forming a section of the drive leading to Clifton Hall, is an ancient prehistoric track. The Grove too, at least in the popular mind, has always been associated with the pagan religion. Sneinton and St Anne's also had its prehistoric track in the form of what is now Porchester Road.

Our first written evidence for the Clifton Maypole comes from 1904, when Lady Bruce, mother of Colonel P.R. Clifton, '.... revived the maypole tradition'. Once again, a permanent pole was sited on the village green. It was over forty feet tall, plain in colour (possibly green, although the information is scant and of course the photographs black and white) and was equipped with a device for lowering and raising a metal ring which during the festivities was decked with green vegetation and flowers. The celebrations took the form of boys and girls dressed in red and white dancing around the pole holding coloured ribbons (also

5: *Clifton May Queen, 1930 (courtesy of Mrs B. Pond).*

possibly red and white) and the crowning of the village May Queen. The pole seems to have stood idle for some years, for we read that in 1912 a revival of May Day festivities was once again made. The 1912 revival lasted between two and four years for either at the outbreak of the Great War or around 1916 May Day festivities ceased at Clifton, as they did in most rural communities. The celebrations may have begun again after the the War. In 1921 we find that not only has Maypole dancing taken place at Clifton but a 'Childrens Festival and a Robin Hood's Day' complete with play has also taken place (shades of the earlier May Days). There must have been yet another period of inactivity, for the local papers of 1937 tell us that; '....a revival of braiding the village maypole at Clifton has been made'. In 1938, Arthur Mee in his *King's England: Nottinghamshire* writes in the entry under Clifton 'Who can forget the green on which every May Day the children dance round the Maypole'.

5a: *Clifton Maypole being carried through the village (undated, probably 1904) (courtesy Nottinghamshire County Libraries.*

At about the same time that Clifton enjoyed its Maypole 'braiding' revival (a term used to describe the form of dancing involving coloured ribbons) plans were being laid for the massive new council estate in the fields opposite the green. Throughout the next few years, letters appeared in the local press for and against the estate (which was, or is, reputed to be the largest of its kind in Europe) with the constant theme of 'Will it affect village life?' With the outbreak of the Second World War, all building plans were put aside and the Maypole was taken down for the duration, as it had been in 1914-18. In 1945, Nottingham's building plans were revived. However, someone forgot to tell the Maypole that the War was over. Although Maypole dancing has taken place on the village green since then, this has been around the small portable poles as used by primary schools. No attempt has ever been made to once again revive the permanent pole.

Farnsfield (Church; Sheet 129 SK 6455650)

It is likely that Farnsfield's Maypole stood on the green opposite the church. As we have already seen, Maypoles were not only used for dancing around on May Day and Farnsfield's pole was no exception. The pole was the focal point for the 'Martinmass Hiring Fair' when farm workers and servants seeking new employment gathered on the green beneath the Maypole to be viewed by prospective employers. The only dated written reference to the pole comes from Howitt's *Rural Life* of 1834 when he states in some disgust that in North Nottinghamshire '....there is a Maypole at Linby and Farnsfield and no other for twenty miles around'. Howitt however, overlooked the poles at Hucknall Torkard and Wellow, both well within this distance.

Gedling (Church; Sheet 129 SK 61814258)

One of the strangest cases in British legal history constitutes our only reference to Gedling's Maypole. The Author of *Calamy's Memorials* (quoted in the County Library's card index file) gives an account of the events but not the date. Sometime early in the reign of Charles I the Rev Truman of Gedling was to have an encounter with a Maypole that was to change his life and cost him a good deal of money. Truman was a prominent member of the community and of the church, a pious Christian with strong orthodox, one might almost say puritanical views. One bright sunny Sunday morning, Rev Truman was riding through the village on his way to visit a sick friend. On passing the village green he saw a group of men and women gathered around the Maypole, preparing it for use. Angered by this, he reined his horse to a halt in order to rebuke these 'wayward souls'. To his surprise, he was greeted by jeers and abuse and told in so many words that they may have been afraid of him once, but now they had the King's writ to be doing what they did. Truman replied, 'You may be obeying the King's Law, but you are not obeying God's'. Truman was so incensed by the incident that he made attempts to have the law regarding Maypoles and the Sabbath changed. To counter this action, those whom he had attempted to rebuke, accused him of inciting them to disobey the King's Law. The whole affair dragged on for nearly a year and cost Truman the then staggering sum of

£1,500. He lost his case and was to die a bitter and broken man. Ironically, his son, Joseph, was removed from his post of rector of Gedling by Oliver Cromwell, the very man who was to almost eradicate Maypoles for ever.

6: *Raising the Maypole eighteenth century style (from Chamber's Book of Days, 1869)*

Gotham (Square; Sheet 129 SK 53603009)

A single reference in the first English book on the subject of blazoning arms constitutes our only evidence for a possible Maypole at Gotham. This reference is repeated in *The Myth of the Pent Cuckoo*, by Rev Field (1913). It connects the Maypole, Robin Hood plays and the decoration of village and pole with pictures of the outlaw's band. 'Gentlemen should not suffer Little John or Much the Miller's sonne to be araied in cotes of arms, as I have seene some wear at Whitsontide in May-pole mirth, which have bin pulled downe and given to them, by the Churchwardens of Gotham'. (*The Accedence of Armorie* by Gerard

Leigh, 1597.) In 1937, Gotham enjoyed a brief and temporary revival of May Day celebrations with a Maypole, May Queen and so forth.

Hucknall Torkard (Pole; Sheet 129 SK 53394939)

Tradition has it that some Linby men stole the Hucknall Maypole before the May Day of 1809. This idea of stealing Maypoles in a sort of inter-village rivalry is a very ancient one and can be found in the history of a number of poles scattered throughout the country. Of this custom, writing in 1660, one puritan writer says 'The most of these May-poles are stollen, yet they give out that the poles are given them... There were two May-poles set up in my parish; the one was stolen, and the other was given by a profest papist. That which was stollen was said to bee given when 'twas proved to their faces that 'twas stollen, and they were made to acknowledge their offence. This pole that was stollen was rated five shillings: If all the poles one with another were so rated, which were stollen this May, what a considerable sum would it amount to! Fighting and bloodshed are usual at such meetings, insomuch that 'tis a common saying, that 'tis no festival unless there bee some fightings'.

The Linby thieves carried off their booty via an ancient footpath that once connected the two villages. We do not know if the Hucknall pole was returned safely before May Day or if, as in the above quote, it led to 'fighting and bloodshed'. The next and final reference we have regarding the Hucknall pole sees it in a state of neglect and decay. Jewitt, in the *Journal of the Archaeological Association* Vol.8, 1853 says 'Maypoles were sometimes very elegantly ornamented and were surmounted by flags and streamers of various colours. One was not many years ago remaining by Hucknall Torkard, and at the top were portions of the iron work and decorations still in being'.

Linby (Pole; Sheet 120 SK 53425099)

The moss-grown cottages, the lowly mansions of grey stone, the Gothic crosses at each end of the village, and the tall Maypole in the centre, transport us in imagination to former centuries.

The quote comes from an American tourist, but not from these dollar-troubled days. The reference is the first written record of Linby's Maypole. It comes from Washington Irving's guide book to *Newstead Abbey and Abbotsford.* The guide was written in 1835, during Irving's stay with the then owner of Newstead, Colonel Wildman. Irving had thought that May Day was dying out in this country as a folk celebration and that little would become of attempts to revive it. Not only did he provide us with our first look at Linby's pole, but went on to view the pole at Wellow and write the first description of a pole at Handbridge, a suburb of Chester.

The life of the Linby pole seems to have been as eventful as any pole in the country. In 1875, the author of *Black's Guide to Nottinghamshire* states 'The lofty maypole so long the pride of the villagers was blown down only a few months ago, and unfortunately has not been replaced". That is not the end of the story however as sometime during the next twelve years the pole was replaced. It is from the year 1887 that we receive our first real description of this truly unique Maypole. The description comes from Alfred Stapleton's wonderful little book, *Crosses of Nottinghamshire, Past and Present*. The pole's inclusion in a book about crosses results from the unique nature of its design and relationship with one of the Linby crosses. 'On visiting Linby in 1887 we saw the Maypole alluded to by Washington Irving, and which we are sorry to find has since disappeared. It was fixed in the ground only about four feet from the base of the Top Cross, of which it appeared to be about three times the height. It was square at the lower part, and about 18" in thickness, but at about the height of 8 feet was cut into octagon form, and the eight sides, as could yet plainly be distinguished, had once been gaily coloured blue and red alternately. It tapered slightly, and seemed to be about 40 feet in height. A long iron clamp about

7:    *Linby Maypole (from Everard L. Guildford's Nottinghamshire, 1910).*

halfway up, marked either where it had been joined or else where a joint had existed for lowering for the purpose of decoration. The lower part of the pole was defaced by bill posters'.

Although in 1887, when Stapleton saw the Linby pole it was in a state of decay and, in fact, subsequently disappeared, it may in fact have been taken down for repair. In 1903 a new pole was erected (or had the old pole once again been restored?). This pole was erected on the traditional site, just four feet from the base of the cross and retained its unique octagonal design. The only apparent difference was that the new pole was painted with a spiral design more familiarly associated with Maypoles. No further mention of the Linby pole being used in May Day celebrations is to be found. The bright new pole of 1903 was once again allowed to lapse into a state of ruinous decay. By 1920 the paint work had flaked and faded. The octagonal base and faded spiral design once again defaced by bill posters can clearly be seen on a photograph taken around this time.

In a newspaper report of 12th June 1920, the reporter is ever uncertain as to whether it is a Maypole or a flagstaff he is writing about. Of the pole he says; 'Associated with the cross is a Maypole or flagstaff, a feature that has lately exchanged its single owner to a number, who it is hoped, will club together and see its retention or preservation. It is still the custom of the village children to dance around a Maypole, but this is a temporary one, erected in the grounds of the rectory'. *Kelly's Directory,* 1922, mentions the pole as still standing. The expected preservation of two years earlier did not come, and whether through lack of funds or interest, the Linby pole finally died after a long illness. Guilford's *Little Guide to Nottinghamshire* (second edition, 1927) declares 'The Maypole at Linby is now but a memory, destroyed in recent years'. The reporter of 1920, quoted above, can be accused of being almost prophetic, for the site of the pole is now occupied by a flagstaff.

The demise of the Linby pole is a particularly sad one. However, before we consign its memory to the annals of history and allow it to rest in peace, a couple of questions beg to be answered. Why was the pole sited so close to the steps of the ancient cross as to make dancing around it almost impossible? Why was the pole a unique, octagonal shape, painted in vertical bands instead of the usual spiral design? I will attempt a short answer to both these questions, but stress that these are theoretical and based on my own understanding of things. With regards to the siting of the pole, Linby was not unique in possessing a pole situated in a position unsuitable for dancing around. A second Nottinghamshire pole, Stapleford, was also sited a few feet from the base of an ancient cross (several Yorkshire poles and a number of others nationally were or are in similar situations). The pole still *in-situ* at Brockworth (Gloucestershire) is sited so close to the precipitous slope of Cooper's Hill as to make dancing around it impossible. The question now arises, were all Maypoles originally meant for dancing around? The answer from this evidence most be 'No!' The Puritan writer Stubbes, clearly defines the Maypole as an idol, an object of religious worship and not merely the phallic symbol we attribute it to be in our post-Freudian world. As an object of religious worship or emblematic of such worship, it stands to reason that it would occupy a site of religious importance to the worshipper.This idea may be somewhat confirmed by the fact that pagan shrines were often sited on high hills and the Cooper's Hill pole is an example of a Maypole on such an eminence. We may also include the pole that once stood in the ancient earthwork on the summit of the hill above the Cerne Abbas Giant, and the giant pole in Stroud in Gloucestershire on the aptly named Pagan Hill. This however does not account for poles like Linby positioned close to an ancient cross. The fact is that where a cross can been shown to be ancient (medieval or earlier), although their association is now christian, they invariably occupy a pagan site. The Maypole may therefore be seen as an attempt to reoccupy as near possible a pagan sacred spot that has been usurped by christianity, as with the erection of a pole in the church yard (see Boughton Maypole). It may also be that the site of the cross and that of the pole are of equal importance. I believe this to be the case at Linby.

As regards dancing around such a pole, the original Maypole dancing was in the form of a 'Ring-around-the-roses' type dance and not the 'ribboning' introduced by Ruskin from Europe in Victorian times. The 'ribboning' form of dance needs more room than merely dancing around the pole in order to achieve the intricate patterns involved. One can envisage perhaps a serpentine dance involving both Maypole and cross. This would invariably lead to the decline of Maypoles like Linby, which, as their original purpose was forgotten and with the introduction of the new form of dancing would become obsolete. To quote once again our reporter friend 'It is still the custom of village children to dance round a Maypole, but this a temporary one, etc. etc.'. The shape of the Linby pole is perhaps a little harder to explain and I will say that I believe it to be no accident, perhaps owing its origin to the ancient art of geomancy. To justify this I will point the reader to the fact that the base of the cross is also octagonal in design with seven steps, an ancient and sacred number. The horizontal paint design is simple, in that the octagonal base of the pole lends itself to such painting, which would in turn emphasis its shape.

I have researched the history of more than three hundred Maypoles throughout the country and, if I were ever to be asked which of the many destroyed and lost poles I would most like to see restored, it would be Linby's. Britain has lost a truly unique piece of its folk history.

North Wheatley (Church; Sheet 129 SK 76198590)

A single reference to Nottinghamshire's most northerly Maypole comes from *Whites Directory* of 1884; 'A feast and hiring for servants are held on the first Thursday in November, when the Green round the lofty maypole is crowded with visitors'. Once again we find a Martinmass Hiring Fair held beneath a Maypole. Perhaps not so surprising when we consider that the pole was on communal open space, the green. But, interestingly, Martinmass is the christianised equivalent to the pagan Celtic Samain which, like May Day Beltane, is one of the four fire festivals. It is even more interesting to note that Samain is at the opposite point of the year to Beltane, and that in a number of cases (Cat Stone for one) where a Beltane sunrise line can be determined, the view in the opposite direction along the alignment gives a Martinmass sunset.

Nottingham (Pole; Sheet 120 SK 57344008)

We do not know if the Nottingham Maypole stood on a traditional site or if the pole mentioned in the City records replaced a former pole. However, it seems likely that the latter was the case.

Sir Charles Sedley, Bart, Gentleman of Nuthall Temple fame, was re-elected to Parliament in 1747. To celebrate his victory it is said that he 'presented his partisans' with the finest fir tree (a larch) in his park at Nuthall, which they erected as the new Maypole. The pole was at the lower end of Parliament Street, close by the junction with Clumber Street, almost opposite the Victoria Centre. It is interesting to note that this site was just outside the medieval city walls, opposite one of the former gates. The pole stood until 1780, long enough to have a public house named after it, (the 'Old Corner Pin' was formerly 'The Maypole'). In 1780, one of the overseers of the highway, Mr Thomas Wyer, declared the pole to be unsafe and ordered it to be taken down. No attempt seems to have been made to replace it and, sadly, both pole and pub have disappeared into history.

Stapleford (Pole; Sheet 120 SK 48903735)

The literal meaning of the name of this ancient village is the ford marked by a 'staple' - a prop, post or a tall shaft. The Stapleford Maypole stood in the middle of the road almost opposite the parish church of St Helen. Only two short references exist regarding the pole and these tell us very little about it. William Stevenson in his *History of Stapleford* tells us that 'The village Maypole at Stapleford was taken down more than sixty years ago, (circa 1810), when the ancient cross was restored'. Alfred Stapleton in his *Crosses of Nottinghamshire* (1903), says that the pole was 'hard by the cross'. Both of these references mention the 'ancient cross'; if we can glean no information about the pole from them, perhaps we can learn something from the history of the cross against which it stood.

8: *Reconstruction of Stapleford Maypole.*

John Holland Walker in *The Stapleford Cross Shaft* (1945) seems to suggest that the village cross at Stapleford was a direct descendant of an ancient stone, either a natural boulder or a monolith, the object of pagan worship. Whatever the origin, most authors agree that Christian worship began on the site of St Helen's church somewhere between 680 - 780 AD. The Domesday Book of 1086 lists a church at Stapleford and an Anglo-Saxon preaching cross of elaborate and ornate design was erected here sometime around 1050 (some authorities say earlier). The shaft of this cross remained in the church yard until 1760, when it was set up in the road by the church on a newly-built stepped base.

Now we can return to our references regarding the pole. Stapleton's 'hard by the cross', indicates that as with Linby, the Maypole must have stood within a few feet of the base of the cross, so close in fact that this necessitated its removal when the base of the cross was remodelled in 1820 (not 1810 as Stevenson states). The question now arises, if the cross was not erected in the middle of the road until 1760, was the Maypole already there? From my own study of Maypoles the logical answer to this question would be 'Yes' a pole did occupy the site pre-1760. Any pole erected after this date on a site not previously occupied or associated with an earlier pole, would, in Maypole terms, be a modern revival and I cannot believe that anyone would choose such an inaccessible site.

9:   Stapleford May Queen, 1924 (courtesy Nottinghamshire County Libraries).

May Day celebrations were to be found in Stapleford long after the Maypole had been forgotten. A photograph, dated 1924, donated to the local library by Mrs I.Towle a native of Stapleford shows a group of school children gathered around what appears to be a large (permanent) Maypole, which may, in fact, be a flagstaff ribboned for the occasion, as the ribbons are merely tied around the post at a height of about fifteen feet, and not attached to a purpose-made bracket. The older girl in the centre of the group is probably the village May Queen. It is unfortunate that no details regarding this photograph have been recorded.

Finally, it is interesting to speculate whether or not it was the Maypole or rather a proto-Maypole as a sacred object that was the 'staple' marking the ford that gave the village its name.

Wellow (Pole; Sheet 120 SK 66956620)

We come now to Nottinghamshire's only remaining permanent Maypole. It is natural, therefore, that the report on this pole should be longer than any of the others, as there is much more information available. The history of the Wellow pole clearly shows something of the social aspect of a Maypole as a landscape feature.

Wellow is a pretty, red brick village, once part of the Rufford Abbey estate. It is partly surrounded by a medieval earthwork, and has the remains of a circular earthwork described as 'probably Norman' nearby. The Maypole stands on a triangular green close to the parish church of St Swithin. We know that there was a Maypole on the village green at Wellow in 1835 as Dean Hole, in *Memories Then and Now*, tells us of the delight of Washington Irving (see also Linby) and later John Leech the artist, at seeing the Maypole at Wellow. How long a pole had stood on this spot we can only hazard a guess, and say that, like Clifton, Wellow has had a pole since 'time immemorial'. It may have been the pole viewed by Irving and Leech that witnessed the celebrational public dinner held on the green in 1856. This was held to commemorate the signing of the treaty with Russia after the war in the Crimea and the pole is mentioned in the account of the dinner.

Some time early in 1860, the pole was sawn down by an inebriated person or persons unknown. A new pole was brought to Wellow, the traditional way, on the shoulders of the villagers, from Pittance Park in Sherwood Forest on the 9th May 1860. A conflicting but interesting and informative report comes the *Folk-Lore Journal* Vol. 2 (1884): 'Passing through the village of Wellow, Notts, a few days ago I saw a maypole in the centre of the village. It was about sixty feet high and had three cross-pieces near the top, at intervals apart. I found that it was a real maypole and had been standing about a quarter of a century; It had replaced an old one which had become rotten and tottering; Many people remember when dancing round the maypole, climbing it when greased, and other games were in full vigour'.

10: Climbing the Maypole (from Chamber's Book of Days, 1869)

Sir John Saville, the owner of Rufford Abbey, gave a new pole to the village of Wellow, on the 22nd June 1887, to celebrate Queen Victoria's Jubilee. This pole was allowed to season in the yard of the Red Lion public house before being erected on the green under the supervision of a Mr Cartlidge, who had also supervised the erection of previous poles. Sir John's pole must have been of good quality, well-seasoned timber, lasting as it did some twenty-three years, finally being replaced in 1910. The new Maypole of 1910 lasted until 1921 and probably would have lasted a lot longer if it had not been burnt down in a freak accident. Fireworks that had been stacked around it ready for a firework party were somehow ignited and the pole literally burnt to the ground. The next pole was to last for twenty-eight years, being taken down in 1949, when it was considered to be in an unsafe condition. Unlike a number of other Maypoles nationally (and at Clifton), I have found no evidence to suggest that Wellow pole was ever taken down during either of the two World Wars. The pole taken down in '1949 was replaced at the beginning of 1950. This pole lasted until 1966 a replacement being erected on the 12th April of that year. This pole had obviously not been 'seasoned' like its predecessors. The weather vane and iron work were removed in October 1974 for restoration and the top third of the pole was found to be badly rotted and decayed. This section was subsequently removed and the Maypole celebrations of 1975 were held using the reduced pole. The present pole is made of steel and is painted with a red, white and blue spiral design. It was supplied by Abacus Municipal of Sutton in Ashfield and was paid for by a grant from Nottinghamshire County Council. It was erected on 7th February, 1976 and stands some 55ft high, approx. 60 ft if the weather vane is included.

11: *Raising Wellow Maypole, twentieth century style (from unsourced newspaper cutting, 1976)*

Maypole celebrations at Wellow are held now on Spring Bank Holiday Monday. I have attended eight such occasions as a member of the Foresters

Morris Men. However, the first time I saw the Maypole dancing here was in 1980, before I joined the Foresters. A brief description of the events (taken from my notes at the time) will serve well as an example of Maypole celebrations nationally as they now appear. In 1980, the Bank Holiday fell on 26th May, some twenty days after May Day, but well within earlier parameters which, after the Restoration, saw Maypoles used any time between the 1st and 29th May (Oak Apple Day).

I had seen Wellow's Maypole on previous occasions and been suitably impressed, but now, seeing it decked with ribbons and surrounded by the hum and anticipation of the waiting crowd, it took on a noble aspect. At the pointed end of the triangular green a stage or platform had been erected and covered with branches of evergreen shrubs. It proved to be the bower for the May Queen. On the opposite side of the green to the village hall an arch of flowers and evergreens had been erected. To the jingle of Morris bells and the sound of a merry tune played on a melodion, the reigning May Queen and her retinue were led from the village hall. They all passed through arches of flowers, mainly artificial, held aloft by small girls. A young boy at the front of the procession blew on a bugle to announce their presence to the waiting audience and led the way round the green and through the arch of evergreens and onto the grass.

Standing on the platform at the end of the green, with due pomp and ceremony, the new May Queen was crowned with a wreath of forget-me-nots by the retiring Queen. After this their majesties were treated to a display of Maypole dancing, given by village children of various age groups. Traditional dances with names like 'Gypsies Tent', 'Barbers Pole', 'Amo Amas' and 'Spiders Web' were exhibited to the delight of the crowd.

Following the Maypole dancers, it was the turn of the Morris Men to exhibit their skills. Led by a man covered with a dark cloth, holding aloft a wooden stag's head with a huge spread of antlers, they danced onto the green. It was in the middle of their display of dancing that the dark clouds which had been over our heads all day like the sword of Damocles, finally broke and the rain lashed down in a sudden torrent. As I scurried back to my car I noticed that another time honoured ritual had been interrupted, the sound of leather on willow had ceased and the cricketers fled the field of ritual combat. Rain had stopped play for us all.

Before leaving the village of Wellow I will say one more thing. It is only by money raised from events as described above that we are able to see and enjoy the English Maypole, for it is such events that pay for their upkeep.

Woodborough (Pole; Sheet 129 SK 63504775)

Although this gazetteer is in alphabetical order, it seems somehow fitting that Woodborough should contribute the final Maypole. Doubtless at sometime in the dim and distant past Woodborough possessed a Maypole in the heart of the old village, but any record of this is not to be found. It is to Nottinghamshire's, and indeed perhaps the country's, newest Maypole that this entry refers. Sadly, the pole had a short and unhappy life and we follow it through from its conception, birth and eventual death.

In 1979, new houses were being built on a greenfield site on the edge of the village, a development known as 'The Pastures'. The pole was erected on a central green on completion of the dwellings by the developers, Costain Homes, and was the brainchild of their own architect. A response to an enquiry from this author in the form of a letter from the then sales director of Costains, Mr A. G. Wheatcroft, tells the story more fully; 'I must confess that this Maypole is essentially decorative and came about as a result of our architect's designing the housing scheme with a central green. It was hoped that the Maypole would be used and become part of the community life'. In spite of the fact that local children of Woods Foundation School were actively engaged in May Day celebrations using a portable 'Continental Maypole' the new 'English Maypole' at Woodborough was never used. On a recent visit to The Pastures, I found that the pole had been removed some two years ago. The pole, like Wellow's, was made of steel and painted with a red, white and blue spiral design. It stood over twenty feet tall and was fully functional in that it had a circular bracket for the attachment of ribbons.

The Band of Hope and 50's Revivalism

Even from Stubbe's time, as early as 1583, it was customary for May Day celebrations to continue through the Whitsuntide period. This change of date, in effect, christianised the old pagan spring festival. The christianisation of May Day or at least, the acceptance of what Stubbes and his fellow puritans considered to be vile pagan anomaly, was complete with its adoption by the Band of Hope Union (an alliance of various chapels who all advocated temperance). In the hands of the chapels, what had once been a rumbustious and riotous occasion became a refined and gentle event. Whitsuntide saw chapel goers gathering in great numbers on village greens and open spaces in fine weather and in village and school halls when the weather was inclement. Continental Maypoles bedecked with flowers and ribbons became the centre of what was essentially a children's occasion.

Just such events, taking place in Nottinghamshire more than fifty years ago, were described to me by Mrs Ward, who was then a native of Westwood, a village in the strong chapel area on the Derbyshire-Nottinghamshire border around Jacksdale. Every chapel (and church) had its own Maypole, around which children in their 'Sunday best' would dance. There would then be a crowning of the May Queen. 'But first we had to all sign the pledge, you know, against drink' said Mrs Ward. Following the dancing and the crowning, all the groups from various chapels would gather together and the whole crowd with bands playing would parade through the streets across the border to the 'Monument' on the hill in Codnor Park. Weather permitting, picnics, hymn singing and games ended an enjoyable day.

The 1950's brought a new post war optimism to Britain and, with the crowning of the Queen, the dawning of a new Elizabethan Age. This in turn fuelled an interest in things regarded as quintessentially English. So it was that a veritable forest of Maypoles (ironically Continental) sprang up every May Day and Whitsuntide. Most primary schools seemed to have gained a pole, not just village schools but what we now regard as inner city schools. While small children were being taught the intricate art of Maypole braiding, a revival of interest in Morris dancing, country dancing and folk singing also became apparent. By the late fifties and early sixties, inter-school braiding contests were being held in many parts of the county and probably, in many other counties too. This 50's revivalism had all the flair and vigour of the Band of Hope, without the religious zeal.

Sadly, many of the poles used then now stand idle in some forgotten corner of a school hall. Perhaps this has something to do with changing taste, or is it more to do with the fact that school teachers who once taught braiding have now retired from the teaching profession without passing on their knowledge to their successors? I do know that even Wellow had trouble a few years ago in finding someone to teach the dances.

If this booklet has served to kindle some interest in May Day and its celebration, or has awakened old memories of former celebrations, then it has fulfilled some of its purpose.

The author would be pleased to receive additional information on traditional Maypoles and can be contacted through the publishers.